Paper Cup MANIA

Christine M. Irvin

Children's Press®

A Division of Scholastic Inc.

New York • Toronto • London • Auckland • Sydney

Mexico City • New Delhi • Hong Kong

Danbury, Connecticut

The author and publisher are not responsible for injuries or accidents that occur during or from any craft projects. Craft projects should be conducted in the presence of or with the help of an adult. Any instructions of the craft projects that require the use of sharp or other unsafe items should be conducted by or with the help of an adult.

Design and Production by Function Thru Form Inc.
Illustrations by Mia Gomez, Function Thru Form Inc.
Photographs ©: School Tools/Joe Atlas

Library of Congress Cataloging-in-Publication Data

Irvin, Christine M.
     Paper cup mania / by Christine M. Irvin
       p. cm. — (Craft mania)
     Includes index.
     ISBN 0-516-22278-3 (lib. bdg.)   0-516-27760-X (pbk.)
     1. Paper work—Juvenile literature. 2. Drinking cups—Juvenile literature.
     [1. Paper work. 2. Handicraft.] I. Title. II. Series.

     TT870 .I7495 2001
     745.5—dc21

                        00-065644

1 2 3 4 5 6 7 8 9 10 R 11 10 09 08 07 06 05 04 03 02

Table of Contents

Welcome to the World of CRAFT MANIA!

Don't throw away that paper cup! Everyday items, such as cardboard tubes and paper plates can become exciting works of art. You can have fun doing the projects in this book and help save the environment at the same time by recycling these household objects instead of just throwing them away.

You can find ways to reuse many things around your home in craft projects. Bottle caps, buttons, old dried beans, and seeds can become eyes, ears, or a nose for an animal. Instead of buying construction paper, you can use scraps of wrapping paper or even last Sunday's comics to cover your art projects. Save the twist ties from bags of bread or vegetables—they make great legs! These are just a few examples of how you can turn garbage into art. Try to think of other things in your home that can be used in your crafts.

♻ Did You Know?

- Each person creates about 4 pounds (1.8 kilograms) of garbage per day.

- Each person in the United States uses about 580 pounds (260 kg) of paper every year. Businesses in the United States use enough paper to circle the earth 20 times every day!

- Americans use enough cardboard each year to make a paper bale as big as a football field.

- Americans throw away more than 60 billion food and drink cans (like tin cans and soft drink cans) and 28 billion glass bottles and jars (like those from ketchup and pickles) every year.

That's a lot of trash!

What you will need

It's easy to get started on your craft projects. The crafts in this book require some materials you can find around your home, some basic art supplies, and your imagination.

Buttons, bottle caps, beads, old dried beans, or seeds for decoration

Glue

Tape

Tempera paints

Colored markers

Hole puncher

Construction paper (or newspaper or scraps of wrapping paper)

Felt (or scraps of fabric)

Twist ties (or pipe cleaners)

You might want to keep your craft materials in a box so that they will be ready any time you want to start a craft project. Now that you know what you need, look through the book and pick a project to try. Become a Craft Maniac!

A Note to Grown-Ups

Older children will be able to do most of the projects by themselves. Younger ones will need more adult supervision. All of them will enjoy making the items and playing with their finished creations. The directions for most of the crafts in this book require the use of scissors. Do not allow young children to use scissors without adult supervision.

☞ Helpful Hints

Small bathroom cups are good for these projects since they usually do not have the wax coating found on the larger cups. Tacky glue will help construction paper and other materials stick to the cups better than regular white glue.

Ancient Pyramid

What you need

- Ten paper cups, all the same size
- Tape
- Glue

What you do

1. Make the base for your pyramid. Arrange six of the cups in a triangle shape, as shown. Use pieces of tape to hold the cups together at the top where they touch each other, as shown.

2 Make the middle layer of your pyramid. Arrange three of the paper cups in a triangle shape like you did in Step 1. Tape them together at the top the same way you did in Step 1.

3 Put your pyramid together. Carefully, turn the six-cup base of your pyramid upside-down. Spread a layer of glue around the rims of the three-cup layer. Turn them upside-down and press them in place on the six-cup base, in the middle, as shown.

4 Spread a layer of glue around the rim of the last cup. Turn it upside-down and press it in place in the middle of the three-cup layer, as shown. Let the glue dry.

Other Ideas

- Add texture to your pyramid. Spread a layer of glue around the sides of your pyramid. Sprinkle sand onto the glue. Let the glue dry completely. Then, tap the loose sand off the paper.

9

Action Figures

What you need

- **One large paper cup for each figure**
- **Pencil**
- **Ruler**
- **Scissors** (Before cutting any material, please ask an adult for help.)
- **Construction paper**
- **Glue**
- **Markers**
- **Small buttons, feathers, or pieces of ribbons**

What you do

1 Give your action figure some legs. Draw two V shapes, each about 2 inches long, on the rim of the cup with the pencil, as shown. The V shapes need to be the same size and they need to be on opposite sides of the cup. Have an adult help you cut out the V shapes.

2 Create clothing for your figure. Have an adult help you cut out strips of construction paper. You can use one thick strip of construction paper to make a uniform or two thinner strips to make different colored pants or skirts and shirts. Make sure each strip of paper is long enough to overlap slightly when you wrap it around the cup. Glue the strip or strips to the cup about 1 inch from the bottom of the cup. Let the glue dry. Trim excess paper from V-shaped openings.

3 Add a head. Turn the cup upside-down. Have an adult help you cut out a strip of construction paper that is 1¾ inch wide, as shown. Make sure the strip of paper is long enough to overlap slightly when you wrap it around the cup. Glue the strip of paper to the cup, about 1 inch down, as shown. Let the glue dry.

4 Give your figure a face. Using the markers, draw eyes, a nose, and a mouth on the strip of construction paper.

5 Add details to the clothing. Glue a piece of ribbon around the middle of your action figure for a belt. Glue two small buttons in place for a shirt. Add other small decorative items to finish the uniform the way you want it. Let the glue dry before playing with your action figure.

Other Ideas

- Use beads, seeds, and scraps of fabric or yarn to decorate your figure's head. Cut out a piece of fabric for the mouth. Glue on yarn for hair and beads or seeds for the eyes and nose.

- Make soldiers instead of action figures. For Navy soldiers, cover the cups in white construction paper. Add belts, buttons, and scarves made from blue construction paper, beads, or scraps of fabric.

Cup Catch Game

What you need

- One large paper cup
- Stick (for a handle)
- Scissors (Before cutting any material, please ask an adult for help.)
- Masking tape
- One 15-inch piece of heavy string
- One ½-inch wooden bead
- Pen

What you do

1. Turn the cup upside-down. Poke a hole in the center of the bottom of the cup with a ball-point pen. Place the stick in the center of the hole.

2 Put a handle on your cup. Wrap several layers of masking tape around the stick, about 1 inch from the end. Push the cup down onto the stick, as shown. Keep pushing until the bottom of the cup touches the masking tape. There should be enough tape wrapped around the stick to keep the cup from falling down over the stick. If the cup still falls over the stick, remove the cup, wrap some more tape around the stick, and try again.

3 Tape one end of the string to the end of the stick inside the cup. Wrap the tape around the stick several times to firmly attach the string.

4 Spread glue around the top edge of the tape. Glue the tape to the hole in the cup. Let the glue dry before going on to Step 5.

5 Thread the other end of the string through the bead. Tie the string into a knot around the bead.

Now you're ready to play the cup catch game. The object of the game is to catch the bead in the cup. This can be tricky. Just keep practicing and have fun with it!

Other Ideas

- Use different sizes of cups and beads to make the game more challenging.

- Decorate your cup. Glue different shapes made from construction paper to the outside of the cup.

Ghoulish Ghost

What you need

- One paper cup
- One white facial tissue or a piece of thin white fabric
- Cotton balls
- Glue
- Markers

What you do

1 Attach cotton balls to paper cup. Turn the paper cup upside-down. Spread a layer of glue around the closed end and sides of the cup. Place several cotton balls in the glue, as shown. Let the glue dry before going on to Step 2.

2 Cover the cup with a facial tissue. Put drops of glue on the cotton balls and the sides of the cup. Place the facial tissue over the top of the cup, as shown. Press the tissue on the top and sides of the cup, making sure to smooth out wrinkles. Let the glue dry.

3 Draw in eyes and a mouth. Use markers to create a face for your ghost. Make sure to draw very lightly on the tissue to prevent it from ripping.

That's it!

Other Ideas

- Use small seeds or beads for a face instead of markers.

- Use newspaper or used wrapping paper to make monsters instead of ghosts.

Telephone Time

What you need

- Two paper cups, the same size
- Pen
- Several feet of lightweight string

What you do

1 Turn the cups upside-down. Using a ballpoint pen, have an adult help you punch holes in the center of the bottom of each cup, as shown.

2 Put your telephone together. Thread one end of the string up through the hole in one of the cups. Tie a knot in the end of the string. The knot needs to be big enough so that it can't fit back down through the hole. Then, do the same thing with the other end of the string and the other cup. The cups will be joined together by the string, as shown.

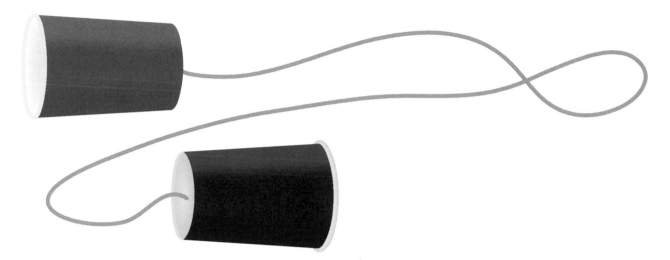

That's it! Your telephone is ready to use. Hold one of the cups up to your mouth, and have a friend hold the other cup up to his or her ear. Make sure that the string is tight. Then talk softly into your cup. Your friend will be able to hear you talking through his or her cup. Take turns talking to each other on your new phone line!

Other Ideas

- Use plastic cups for your telephone instead of paper cups.

- Experiment with different lengths of string to see how far apart you and your friend can talk on your telephone.

Radical Robot

What you need

- One paper cup
- Aluminum foil
- Glue
- Two small buttons (for eyes)
- Small scraps of colored paper or felt (for nose and mouth)
- Twist ties or pipe cleaners (for arms and antennae)
- Scissors (Before cutting any material, please ask an adult for help.)
- Construction paper

What you do

1 Wrap the cup in aluminum foil. Measure a piece of aluminum foil big enough to cover one paper cup from top to bottom. Have an adult help you cut the foil. Then, wrap the foil around the cup, as shown. Fold down the edges of the foil at the top and bottom of the cup to hold it in place.

2 Give your robot a head. Turn the paper cup upside-down. Spread a thick layer of glue on the bottom of it. Crumple a piece of aluminum foil into a ball. Press the foil ball into the glue, as shown. Let the glue dry before going on to Step 3.

3 Give your robot a face. Glue the buttons in place on the head for eyes. Have an adult help you cut shapes from the paper or felt for a nose and mouth. Glue them in place on the robot's face. Let the glue dry before going on to Step 4.

4 Add the antennae and the arms. Glue two twist ties to the paper cup for arms. Bend another twist tie into a V shape and glue it to the top of the head. Let the glue dry before going on to Step 5.

5 Finish your robot. Draw designs on construction paper to decorate the robot's body. Have an adult help you cut out the shapes. Glue the shapes onto the cup. Let the glue dry before playing with your robot.

Other Ideas

- Use small metal bolts and washers for the face instead of buttons and fabric.
- Make an alien. Cover the cup in green construction paper and use a ball of colored plastic wrap for the head.

Magical Mini-Garden

What you need

- Seven paper cups, the same size
- Large polystyrene tray
- Masking tape
- Potting soil
- Pebbles
- Plant seeds

What you do

1. Place the cups on the foam tray with one cup in the center and the other six cups around it. Tape the cups together, as shown.

2 Place pebbles on the bottom of each cup. The pebbles will allow the soil to drain any excess water.

3 Decide what types of plants you want to grow in your mini-garden. Fill the cups about ¾ full with potting soil. Sprinkle a few seeds in each cup. Cover the seeds with a thin layer of potting soil. Sprinkle some water on top of the soil, just enough to make the soil damp.

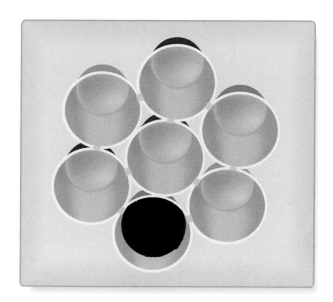

4 Place the tray in a sunny spot indoors. Water the soil every day until your seeds sprout.

Other Ideas

- Plant flower seeds to make a flower garden.
- Plant herb seeds, such as mint and oregano, to make a kitchen garden.

Speedy Locomotive

What you need

- One bath tissue tube
- Two small boxes, such as empty gelatin boxes
- Glue
- Two small paper cups
- Six large, flat buttons (for wheels)
- Four toothpicks

What you do

1. Spread a layer of glue on one side of one of the gelatin boxes. Press the two gelatin boxes together, as shown, to make a bigger box. Let the glue dry before going on to Step 2.

2. Attach the bath tissue tube to the boxes. Spread a layer of glue around one end of the bath tissue tube. Press the boxes in place on the end of the tube, as shown. Let the glue dry before going on to Step 3.

3 Add a paper cup to the bath tissue tube. Spread a layer of glue around the other end of the tube. Press the paper cup in place over the end of the tube, as shown. Let the glue dry before going on to Step 4.

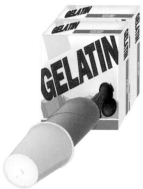

4 Add a smokestack. Spread a layer of glue around the rim of the other cup. Turn the cup upside-down and glue it to the bath tissue tube, as shown. Let the glue dry before going on to Step 5.

5 Add the wheels. Spread some glue on one of the buttons. Press it in place on the bottom of your locomotive. Glue the other five buttons in place for the other wheels, three wheels on each side. Let the glue dry before going on to Step 6.

6 Connect the wheels. Put a dab of glue on each end of one of the toothpicks. Press the toothpick in place across two of the wheels. Glue another toothpick across the last wheel. Turn the locomotive around and glue the other tooth-picks across the other wheels. Let the glue dry before playing with your locomotive.

Other Ideas

- Paint the bath tissue tube and gelatin boxes with tempera paints.
- Cover the bath tissue tube and the gelatin boxes with construction paper before gluing them together in Step 2.

Wild Windsock

What you need

- One paper cup
- Plastic shopping bag
- Scissors (Before cutting any material, please ask an adult for help.)
- Glue
- Hole puncher
- One 12-inch piece of string

What you do

 Have an adult help you cut the plastic bag into strips about 12 inches long.

2 Spread a layer of glue around the inside of the cup. Press the strips of plastic into the glue, as shown. Let the glue dry before going on to Step 3.

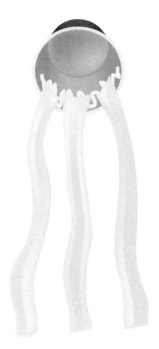

4 Add a hook. Punch two holes in the side of the cup, one on each side. The holes need to be across from each other. Thread one end of the string through one hole and the other end of the string through the other hole, as shown. Tie the two ends of the string, as shown.

3 Have an adult help you cut out the bottom of the paper cup.

5 Hang your windsock in a windy place.

Other Ideas

- Use a plastic cup instead of a paper cup. The plastic cup will last longer outside than a paper cup.

- Decorate your windsock for the seasons. Use flowers for spring, bright colors for summer, leaves for fall, and snowflakes for winter.

Colorful Kaleidoscope

- One small paper plate
- Pencil
- Scissors (Before cutting any material, please ask an adult for help.)
- Glue
- Scraps of colored plastic wrap or cellophane
- One large paper cup
- Pen

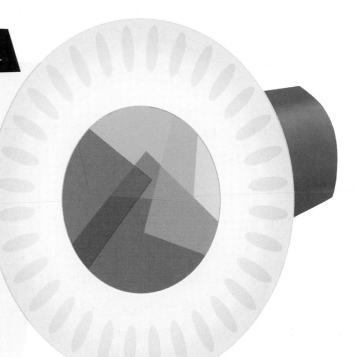

What you do

1. Using the pencil, draw a circle in the center of the paper plate. Have an adult help you cut out the circle, as shown.

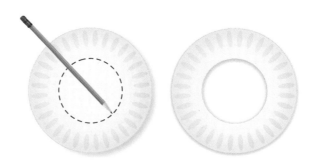

2 Glue scraps of colored plastic wrap over the hole you cut out of the paper plate. Let the glue dry before going on to Step 3.

3 Using a ballpoint pen, have an adult help you punch a hole in the bottom of the cup.

4 Put your kaleidoscope together. Spread a layer of glue around the rim of the paper cup. Press the paper plate in place on the paper cup, as shown. Let the glue dry before playing with your kaleidoscope.

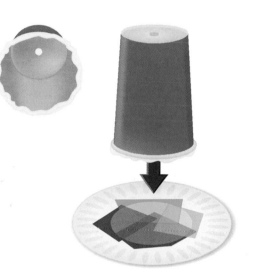

Hold the bottom of the paper cup up to your eye. Look through the hole in the bottom of the cup as you turn the cup to make the colors change.

Other Ideas

- Decorate the outside of your kaleidoscope. Cover the cup with white construction paper and use markers or crayons to make interesting designs.

Clara the Chicken

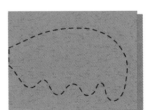

What you need

- **One paper cup**
- **Construction paper** (for the comb, wings, tail, and beak)
- **Pencil**
- **Scissors** (Before cutting any material, please ask an adult for help.)
- **Glue**
- **Two small buttons** (for eyes)

What you do

1. Make the wings. Have an adult help you cut a rectangle from a piece of construction paper. Fold the rectangle in half. Starting at the fold, draw a wing shape. With the paper still folded, cut out the wing shape. Then cut the wing at the fold, as shown. This gives you two even-sized wings.

2. Make a comb and a tail for your chicken's body. Draw a comb shape on the paper with the

pencil, as shown. For the tail, trace a rectangle on the paper. Have an adult help you cut out these two shapes.

3 Make a beak. Have an adult help you cut out a diamond shape from the construction paper.

4 Add wings to the cup. Fold under the straight edge on the end of the wings about ¼ inch. Spread a thin layer of glue on the folded edge of the wing. Turn the cup upside-down and glue the wings in place, one on each side of the chicken's body, as shown.

5 Add the chicken's comb. Fold under the straight edge of the comb about ¼ inch. Spread a thin layer of glue on the folded edge of

the comb. Glue the comb in place on top of the chicken's head.

6 Add the tail. Fold the tail like you are going to make a fan, as shown. Pinch one end of the fan and fold under the paper about ¼ inch. Glue the pinched part of the tail in place on the back of the chicken's body. Hold until the tail begins to stick to the cup.

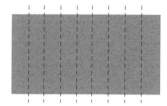

7 Give your chicken a face. Fold the diamond shape in half. Glue the beak in place, as shown. Glue the two buttons in place for eyes. Let the glue dry before playing with your chicken.

Other Ideas

- Make a family of chickens using different sized cups.

Wonderful Windmill

What you do

1 Make the blades. Using the pencil, draw windmill blade shapes on the paper plate, as shown. Have an adult help you cut out the blade shapes.

2 Punch a hole in the middle of the paper plate. Use the hole puncher to make a hole in the end of the straw. Push the end of the paper fastener through the hole in the blades and then through the hole in the straw, as shown. Fasten the ends of the paper fastener loosely so the blades will turn on the straw.

3 Using a ballpoint pen, have an adult help you poke a hole in the bottom of the paper cup. Turn the cup upside-down. Spread a layer of glue around the hole.

4 Push the end of the straw down through the hole in the cup, as shown. Hold the straw in place until the glue sets. Let the glue dry before playing with your windmill.

Other Ideas

- Make your windmill with a polystyrene plate and a plastic cup and use it for an outside garden decoration.

Index

About the Author

Christine M. Irvin lives in the Columbus, Ohio area with her husband, three children, and dog. She enjoys writing, reading, doing arts and crafts, and shopping.